Light Beams

Also by Valerie June Hockett

Maps of the Modern World

Light Beams

A WORKBOOK FOR BEING YOUR BADASS SELF

Valerie June Hockett

Andrews McMeel
PUBLISHING®

Andrews McMeel Publishing
a division of Andrews McMeel Universal
1130 Walnut Street, Kansas City, Missouri 64106

www.andrewsmcmeel.com

23 24 25 26 27 IGO 10 9 8 7 6 5 4 3 2 1

ISBN: 978-1-5248-7850-4

Illustrations: Valerie June Hockett

Editor: Patty Rice
Art Director: Holly Swayne
Production Editor: Brianna Westervelt
Production Manager: Shona Burns

ATTENTION: SCHOOLS AND BUSINESSES
Andrews McMeel books are available at quantity discounts with bulk purchase for
educational, business, or sales promotional use. For information, please e-mail the
Andrews McMeel Publishing Special Sales Department: sales@amuniversal.com.

This Workbook belongs to an Iridescent and

Brightly Fluorescent Badass Named:

X: _____

I AM THE STARS
YOU ARE THE MOONSHINE
AND IF YOUR LIGHT'S RUNNING LOW
YOU CAN BORROW FROM MINE.

—Electric Moonbeam Transfer

Introduction

The purpose of manifesting dreams is to learn to mindfully engage with all of existence. Every path we take can lead us either to harmony or hardship. While I adore books and themes that keep me focused on generating more success in life, with every personal achievement there is a lesson that motivates me to search for deeper ways of expanding the joy, beauty, and benevolence the universe has shared with me. Besides, what is the point if our successes and achievements fail to extend positively beyond our personal spheres?

In a time when wellness and self-improvement have become a $4.5 trillion-dollar industry, many of us are seeking a more profound spiritual solution for sustainable change. From crystals to magic potions, meditations, and yoga, we are spending billions of dollars, yet we are still hungry for true wellness. The truth is wellness cannot be purchased at our local health-food store. Wellness and mindfulness are actions. It is how we relate to one another at the grocery store, in line at the coffee shop, or as we sit impatiently in traffic. It's how we relate to nature and our environment. Stores are lined with shelves of books that tell you how following *your* dreams and being a badass can bring *you* beaucoup money, power, fame, or success. But isn't the act of manifesting those things ultimately a form of proving to ourselves that we can accomplish almost anything with the right skills, talent, and timing? If so, then collectively, WE and only we are responsible for the world as we know it. If we wish to end world hunger, have more respect for the planet, educate the masses, balance racial and gender inequalities, alleviate poverty, or address any of the other global issues facing the world today, the same tools for manifesting individual dreams can be used by all of us collectively to shift the trajectory of our planet in positive ways. We have the power. We are the ones we have been waiting for. Every day is an opportunity to send light beams of empathy, love, and inspiration across the sky like rocket ships around the moon.

So, what does it take to recognize our superpowers and activate them for good?

While the systemic imbalances we face every day keep us all in chains and ties, bound to layers of antiquated practices and policies, the average person hardly has a moment to examine the underlying layers beyond race, gender, and beliefs that are rapidly unraveling the world as we know it.

While horror stories are featured in the media and told with little care for simultaneously highlighting mindful and empathic possibilities for solutions, we constantly live on code red with fear-based thinking as our first response.

While we, the masses, feel unrepresented and have chosen to pick numbness and chill — thinking we have no way to implement actual, true change — it is here we find ourselves facing three of the most significant challenges known in the existence of humanity.

1. A Global Climate Crisis
2. The Technological Hacking of the Human Mind and Body
3. The Daily Threat of Nuclear War

Looking to the golden rule, do unto others as you would have them do unto you, how much is the future of technology influenced by how we treat one another? As algorithms learn our patterns, how do our interactions and views of others shape how we, in turn, might be treated in the coming times? As facial scanners learn to read our minds by examining the expressions on our faces, how will it even be possible to have or conceal an opinion that we currently call a democratic right? With our conversations dominated by gender, race, and beliefs, what will these battles mean when we've all been made equal by unfortunate circumstances?

We currently live in a technologically advancing world eager to explore the consciousness, emotions, and thoughts of our minds. The data collected could be used humanely, for healing, or to create harm. We could use it to bring us together or to tear us apart. There has never been a more critical time in history to examine ourselves and our relationship to those we may not 100% relate to, agree with, or even share the same ideas. There has never been a more crucial time to strip ourselves of prejudices. Now is the time to see ourselves as a multicultural united human family — rich or poor, old or young, black or white.

It is a treasure to be a human — a perfectly imperfect being. Still, when it comes to cultivating unity and togetherness, we have never seen a more crucial time in the history of humankind than now. Now is the time to train ourselves to be more compassionate. Now is the time to practice empathy. As scientists sculpt AI technology behind closed doors in angel white lab coats, we must ask ourselves: Who do we want to be? How would we like to be treated in a world where we coexist with super-intelligent beings? Superior beings. Supreme beings. The brightest. The fastest. The best. The thought processes we adhere to now are the qualities and virtues that shape the creations of our technological future. After hacking the gold, oil, and reservoirs of our minds, will we then question the need for the wealthiest 1% to even keep a semblance of humanity present on the planet? Why will they even need us? What will it mean to pit race against race to uphold the illusionary benefits of white supremacy? There would no longer be a need for the masses to keep this centuries-long charade of social division going. Everyone will be an underdog. Everyone will be a negro. Everyone will search for a crumb at the heel of the wealthiest shoe. So then, what will our gender, age, or beliefs matter? What will be the value of human life in a world of superior intelligence? What does it mean to be a human beyond the constructs of race, class, or gender? Who do we want to be? How do we want to relate to one another?

Well, maybe we're f*cked. Maybe we won't be able to reduce emissions and our dependence on fossil fuels. Though scientists continuously show us ways to change, maybe it will be too late to avoid or even limit some of the worst effects of climate change. Maybe it doesn't matter if we pollute the planet with plastic from sea to shining sea. After all, Mother Earth is a survivor. What we know of ancient human civilizations is that they have been fleeting. But who are we and who do we want to be in this experiment called humanity? If these are our last days, then what would it be like to spend them encouraging togetherness instead of tearing each other apart?

Since the creation of the atomic bomb, we've lived with the threat of nuclear extinction. Maybe one day, a maniac will escalate matters, and perhaps it will end humanity as we know it. Who do we want to be in the face of these threats of destruction? How do we want to leave the planet? Though many of the solutions are out of our personal control, is it possible for us to bind together in communities worldwide to leave this place with a more harmonious spirit than we found it?

How do we begin to claim a new story and shape a new narrative?

What if it's as easy as starting where we are? We are already sitting in the seat of abundance. What if we begin with the revolutionary act of kindness? What if we start by calling into existence a language of joy that will allow the hearts of others to be motivated and inspired to dream a new story alongside us? Who is responsible for growth and change if we aren't?

As a friend said to me, we live in a time when everyone thinks they are "woke," but the plastic is there—and it's not my fault. The atrocities of the past, from brutalities of colonization and slavery, happened, but that wasn't me either. The present injustices, the confinement of living in a patriarchal society, or the strain of upholding white supremacy exists, but I don't believe it's my fault either. We live in a time where we've evolved to acknowledge the past transgressions and the present injustices, but it wasn't me. So, what does it look like to take responsibility? What does it look like to own a personal contribution to these systems that stifle us all—every gender, every race, and every class? If you were a human born on planet Earth, you are responsible for the state of things—past, present, or future. Our power is now. Though humanity comes from barbaric roots, there has never been a more peaceful time in the history of humankind than now. We live in a sliver of time that allows us to explore our potential for positivity and to sculpt a kinder, gentler world. Opportunities for beauty are everywhere in our everyday encounters. In recovery, they say the first step is admitting you have a problem. It is beautiful to see us awakening to that admission of responsibility and beginning to dream new dreams.

To many people, believing in dreams in a world full of harshness can seem like we are being too soft and naive, thinking that we can meditate our way to a healthier planet. Our ears are fine tuned to a language of war. As the Vietnamese-American poet Ocean Vuong mentions, we are still very primitive in the way we speak and value ourselves through the lexicon of death. Using phrases like "you're killin' it," "battleground states," "you slayed," we have been trained in the language of war. But what would it look like to speak into existence a language of joy and harmony? Historian Yuval Noah Harari and philosopher Joseph Campbell speak about the power of stories and myths. Yuval talks about how many things in our society are based on collective belief in stories. He says money is just paper, but it is real because we *believe* it can be used for trading and buying us real things like a banana at the store. Because we *believe* in the idea of America, it is real. Because we collectively *believe* in democracy, it is real, but these are all just fictional stories we have collectively dreamed up and willed into manifestation. The stories and narratives we mutually believe were once only dreams. Many things attempt to dumb down our dreams, hopes, creativity, and imagination. Distracting people from their magic is a way of dimming their power. Is there an art to living magically, and how can it help us to write new stories? Where does it begin? Who does it begin with? What dreams do we share as a collective? The exercises and prompts in this book boldly reclaim our right to be a light in a world that constantly robs us of the currency of our imaginations, wonder, and dreams. There is power in radical imagination. The light beams of our collective dreams have the power to be as bright as the summer sun.

This gorgeous planet Earth is rich with a badass collective of humans with the power to dream. And yes, we are the dreamers we have been waiting for. Spending even a few seconds focusing on brightness transforms our everyday experiences. So, let's fire up the engines and alert ground control that it's time to blast off to a phosphorescent realm of luminescence.

May you shine and shine brightly!

Love,

V. June

LIGHT BEAM
VISUALIZATION EXERCISE

In opening this book, sit in a comfortable place and begin to bring your
awareness to your breath. Take as long as you'd like just following each
breath in and out. When you are ready, invite a light of any color to surround
your entire body, head to toe. Visualize the light sparkling, shimmering,
and swirling all around you. Continuing to follow your breath, extend your
compassionate light to your inner circle of loved ones first, then to your
neighbors and town, and lastly to the entire planet. Uplift all living
creatures with light beams. Feel free to share those sparks and beams for as
long or as short of a time as you're moved to. Imagine with each breath your
light is becoming brighter and brighter.

Welcome to this inquisitive journaling exploration meant to examine and reignite a curiosity for your sweetest self. Engaging colors, mantras, agreements, maps, wishes, observations, and spells, these activities will strengthen and enrich the beauty that already radiates from you just being YOU! Any and everything can be recreated and there's nothing new under the sun, but for always and forever, there is only one YOU! So, get ready to get busy being your badass self.

"Do I contradict myself?
Very well, then I contradict
myself, I am large,
I contain multitudes."

—Walt Whitman, "Song of Myself"

No exact same footprint
Has ever been made in the sand
There's something fiercely powerful—
To be who you are, knowing where you stand

There's no breath that gently settles
In the air or on the wind
That has passed this way before
Or may venture here again

And our lives—as if they're numbered
Receive just seconds in the sun
While some wish and hope for longer
Like a light switch, all drift on.

Living lantern, fleeting moments
Little light through countless forms
Blinking—all's been but a flicker
Present moment, newly born

—LIVING LANTERNS

From the sun to the moon and the stars, there are many shades and sources
of light, but light from every angle is never exactly the same. If you and
a friend are looking at the same lamp, you will not see it in the exact
same way because your friend can never be YOU. They will never be sitting
in the exact same place or viewing from the exact same angle as you. Not
to mention how the weight of each person's past, and even the weight of
a single day's events, might affect and shape the way they perceive the
world. Each view is unique and gorgeous in its own right.

While radiant moments can be shared, every experience of life and light is
uniquely different for every person. How can your perspectives, thoughts,
or views help positively affect the lives of those around you?

INCANDESCENT MOON BATH AND STARGAZING EXERCISE

Sit with a friend and gaze up at the moon and stars. They are the lanterns of the night sky. Describe what you see. Highlight any differences or similarities you observe. While soaking in bright moonbeams, celebrate the uniqueness of who you are. Respect the differences and observations your friend shares with you. Appreciate the time you have together for this exercise. Life will hopefully allow you to share many more moments just like this one, but even that will not be the same. You'll be a little older, probably wearing another outfit, and maybe even a little wiser.

BADASS RESPECT MANTRA FOR FRIENDSHIP AND HUMANITY

The badass in me respects and appreciates the badass in you. Although we see the world through different lenses, I honor your views and perspectives. Thank you for being. Thank you for sharing.

I love to see you brightly shining.

I love celebrating the diversity of our world.

Now, extend this viewpoint to strangers. The next time you're in a busy area for people-watching, observe the differences you may have from those passing by. Although we are all different, notice any similarities and things you have in common. Write down a few things you appreciate about them. This can be something they are wearing, their hairstyle, skin tone, accent, or the shape of their nose. How cool is it that your life is filled with so many interesting humans all living in their own little microcosmic worlds?!

Observations of Appreciation

For each person that passes, gently whisper and extend the Badass Respect Mantra for Friendship and Humanity to every stranger. There are too many people on earth to become close friends with them all, so this mantra radiates well wishes for all living beings. In the same way a smile can change a person's demeanor, a badass knows that whispering wishes for well-being can begin to shift the moods and attitudes of others, too.

*EXTRA CREDIT
MANTRA EXTENSION EXERCISE

From the coffee shop to an airport, we spend much of our lives waiting in
line. For a little extra credit, the next time you find yourself queued up
in a line, practice repeating the Badass Respect Mantra for Friendship and
Humanity for each person ahead of you. It's a way to put your mindfulness
in motion, and the line might even appear to be moving faster. No matter
what, you'll be standing there cultivating patience and radiating calmness
while practicing your Jedi light-magic mantra tricks!

"To be yourself in a world that is constantly trying to make you something else is the greatest accomplishment."

—Ralph Waldo Emerson

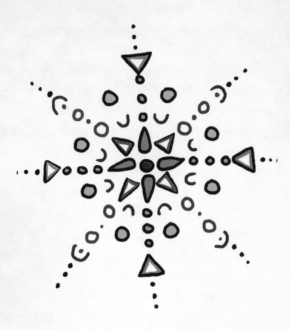

LIGHT BEINGS
MUST BE LIKE THE SUN NEVER ASKING—SHOULD I SHINE?
EVER KNOWING—THAT TO SHINE
IS SIMPLY TO SHOW UP
IRIDESCENTLY
BEING
WHO THEY ARE.

—Who Are You?

Illuminated Image
Collection Exercise

What gives you light? Collect ten to twenty photos that give you light.
Photos that make you smile, laugh, cry, or feel something magical.

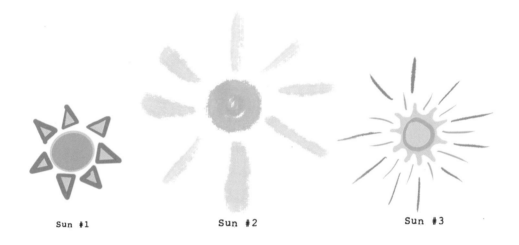

Sun #1   Sun #2   Sun #3

Look for images that inspire you. Glance at these images once a day. Begin
by quickly scrolling or flipping like you're looking at a social media
feed or movie. This exercise should only last for one to three minutes.
It's important to have exercises like this one in order to keep your energy
levels charged up and ready to share light with others. You can use it
as a power booster to begin your day or when you hit a low moment in the
day. Although you should feel free to collect more images and expand the
exercise, it's a-okay to keep it as a short and powerful energy booster.
After all, you're a badass with a pretty long to-do list of the daily tasks
it takes to be a human!

"In nature we never see anything isolated, but everything in connection with something else which is before it, beside it, under it, and over it."

—Johann Wolfgang von Goethe

healing

sweetness

Kindness

JOY

happiness

PRotection

Whether we are drinking a cup of tea or dancing to a bumping song, every
action made affects the entire planet in one way or another. All things are
interwoven and connected. The greatest thing about sharing your uniqueness
with others is that though we are all different, no one is more special
than anyone else. We are all unicorns! We're all in this thing together
and, hopefully, just trying to find ways to grow and peacefully coexist
every day.

Sharing our light takes daily practice. Use this Light Practitioner's Visualization Agreement to list three ways you envision yourself being able to contribute something wonderful to the world.

LIGHT PRACTITIONER'S VISUALIZATION AGREEMENT

I, _____,

vow to spend my earth days doing _____,

_____, and

_____

for others in hopes of leaving the planet sweeter, kinder, and more loving than I found it. I know I will not touch every heart, but I believe every life has the potential to share at least one gift with its immediate sphere that can radiate out into the world.

I vow to be a light practitioner.

Sign: _____

Print: _____

As of this Date: _____

—A Life of Purpose/Light Practitioner's Agreement

"All things are bound together. All things connect."

—CHIEF SEATTLE

"If you want to be happy for a year, plant a garden; if you want to be happy for life, plant a tree."

—English proverb

IF YOU TAKE YOUR WORRIES
AND GO DEEP
WITHIN THE FOREST
SILENT—TALK WITH TREES
REMEDY
TO SEE YOU'RE BLESSED
JUST A WALK WITH TREES
HEALING BALM
WHO WOULD HAVE GUESSED?!

—Tree Therapy

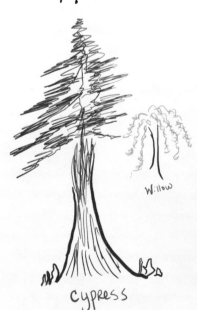

Palm

Willow

Cypress

TREE THERAPY SPELL

What are a few of your most repetitive worries? These can be worries you have about yourself, the future, the past, your family, the world, or damn near anything.

Now, write down the names of your top five favorite trees.

Beside the name of each tree, list a place nearby where you might be able to go visit one or two of your ancient, wise tree friends.

On a day that's convenient for you, venture out for a walk to whisper your worries to a favorite tree. You will find that you don't even have to open your mouth to speak. Ancient tree language is silent, yet always understood. Give your worries to the tree and trust that it is strong enough to carry the burdens and load on your behalf. Even just a few seconds of presence and awareness in the company of a favorite tree, will send light beams of iridescent positivity piercing through the ether for all those who are in tune to revel and bask in! Happy Forest Bathing!

Top Five Favorite Trees:

1.

2.

3.

4.

5.

"ALL PLANTS ARE OUR
BROTHERS AND SISTERS AND
THEY TALK TO US AND IF WE
LISTEN WE CAN HEAR THEM."

—Native American proverb

WHAT'S THE STORY, MORNING GLORY?
HOW DO YOU RISE AND SHINE SO BRIGHT?
PLEASE SHARE YOUR SECRETS OF HOW TO CLING
TO THE RIGHT THINGS
AND HOW TO KEEP GROWING
TOWARD THE LIGHT
WHAT'S THE STORY, MORNING GLORY?
HOW DO YOU TAKE
SOMETHING TIGHTLY CLOSED AND BLUE
AND WAKE SO OPEN EVERY MORNING
AFTER THE DARKNESS OF NIGHT
WITH A BRIGHT, IRIDESCENT HUE?

—*Ode to the Morning Glory*

Plants are our greatest teachers. They have a continuous conversation with the light. For example, a morning glory plant will open with the morning sun and close at night like a shopkeeper at quittin' time. The lesson of the morning glory plant is to know when to rest and how to gently awaken as you feel rejuvenated and ready to face the sunrise. For those who shine brightly, it's a-okay to rest your glow. Have you learned any lessons from plants? It may be watching from your living room window as a tree changes with the seasons, fighting with a pesky weed that keeps growing in the sidewalk, or simply a lesson taught by observing the growth of your front lawn. Who are your favorite plant teachers? What messages are your favorite plant guides sharing with you? List a few of your favorite plant teachers.

_____

_____

_____

_____

_____

_____

_____

_____

_____

_____

_____

_____

_____

_____

_____

"To see a World in a Grain of Sand
And a Heaven in a Wild Flower
Hold Infinity in the palm of your hand
And Eternity in an hour"

—William Blake, "Auguries of Innocence"

Everywhere's a here.
Be busy
Blooming
Where you are
Planted.
This moment is always now.
Breathe in
Taking nothing for
granted.

—To Be Here Now

MOMENTS OF WHOLENESS AND HAPPINESS

What are those moments of mystery that happen when you feel complete and total happiness? I mean, a bliss parade!

They seem to be a blink in the chaos we call life. They often shock us by lasting only a breath or two, so what does an observation of those exact moments look like? Sure, everyone says to "live in the moment" or "carpe diem," but what does that even mean?

This is an exercise in riding the waves of those half-second moments of bliss, blessings that creep in despite the madness, challenges, or disappointments held within a regular day.

Let's start with an awareness and a commitment to observing your thoughts today as if you were watching a leaf blow in the wind. If things appear calm, just observe. If there's a dreaded shitstorm brewing, just watch as the winds of the tornado sweep you away. But if you happen to catch yourself floating on a cloud of "I'm so damn lucky!," then fully embrace that glimpse into heaven as if it were gelato after a heatwave.

Allow that luckiness and happiness to expand. Is anything making it a special moment, or are you just on a rocket ship to Bowie-land? Scribble down any special sparks here:

_____

_____

_____

_____

_____

_____

_____

_____

_____

_____

_____

_____

_____

_____

_____

_____

_____

_____

_____

_____

_____

_____

_____

_____

_____

_____

Is there anything you can list in your present vicinity to embellish your moment of bliss? A flower? A color? A texture or smell? Allow yourself to accessorize your bliss by finding little things that lead you to higher and higher levels of exuberance. Release any guilt or worries that may arise around enjoying this tiny-dancing time of wonder. You deserve it, and we all know it ain't gonna last forever! Part of living on earth is the rise and fall and balance of bliss with obstacles. You might as well levitate and glow when life's moments allow you to soar. It's a gift. Celebrate!

1.

2.

3.

Are there any blissful moments from the past that could be cataloged alongside this glimpse into a galaxy of brightness? If so, jot down those memories:

_____

_____

_____

_____

_____

_____

_____

_____

_____

_____

_____

_____

_____

_____

Are there any hopeful wishes for the future that would keep
these sparks of joy crackling?

_____

_____

_____

_____

_____

_____

_____

_____

_____

_____

_____

_____

_____

_____

_____

_____

_____

_____

_____

_____

_____

_____

Soar in these thoughts. Allow your imagination to take you away just for a few seconds to where the bliss of this moment reigns endlessly—beyond time, beyond space, vastly lasting forever in its own realm of jubilation. Believe me when I tell you it's alright to wake up years later as if you'd fallen into a realm within this realm, basking in the beauty and boundless potential for something unexpectedly gorgeous. Believe that it's a-okay to practice living in the realm of hope, wonder, and imagination.

And congratulations, you have just expanded and multiplied a moment of bliss. Your bliss and joy are superpowers that are always with you even in the darkest storm. In practicing over time, just watch as you slowly begin to find yourself able to carry these sparks from seconds, minutes, and hours, to days, weeks, months, and maybe even traveling through light years! Being able to do this practice is especially important to help balance life's lows. It can be hard to believe brighter days are ahead when you wake up and feel like shit, but a badass learns to dance through it all . . . both the gold and the grit.

"FOREVER — IS COMPOSED
OF NOWS —"

—Emily Dickinson

Said one soul to another
In the ether's waiting room (before birth):
Oh, you're going to earth?!
It can be very dark sometimes,
But there are reflections everywhere
To remind you that you always carry
An inner light— A glimmer on a glass,
The glistening of a water droplet,
The shine of your house keys,
An opening of the sun
Seen through a crowd of tree leaves,
The glowing of a beetle's back,
The smooth inner surface of a seashell
All filled with reflective rays
To help you remember
To look for the brightness in all your days.

—One Soul to Another

The sun
Never stops shining
Though we cannot always
See its glow
This is worth
Remembering
In the times when we're
Feeling low.

—Bright Beam Battery

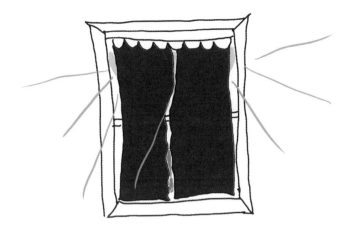

Look for the Light Exercise

Find a comfortable position in one of your favorite rooms. Make sure it's either daytime or the light is on in the room. Make a list of all the corners and crevices where you see light. Is there any light reflecting off other surfaces? Write down any rainbow reflections, any objects, or shades of light that fill the room around you. Simply become aware of the light that surrounds you.

1.

2.

3.

4.

5.

"It is during our darkest moments that we must focus to see the light."

—ARISTOTLE

EXTRA TIDBITS OF INNER SELF-INSPIRED WISDOM
AND KNOWLEDGE:

Jot down any tidbits or lessons you can learn from your light observations.

EXAMPLE: Usually, I don't take notice of the light in my room, but today, as the hours passed, I noticed the softness and subtlety of each movement. The light took its time traveling throughout the day. I thought of how I am always in a hurry. I put on a record and was inspired to dance in slow motion across the room while letting the light guide the way! I danced for those who are struggling. I danced for those who have a day so busy that they can't take a moment to shake it all off. I danced as a way of using my time and body for just a second to carve out a few moments of joy. I danced because joy is a choice. This is a path to freedom.

*Note to self: Just like the light, I will get to where I'm going in the perfect amount of time. Keep shining!

_____

_____

_____

_____

_____

_____

_____

_____

_____

_____

This exercise is a reminder that beams of light can be found in the strangest of places, it just depends on where you're focused. Look for the light in all your days. You can take this exercise with you to almost anywhere you might wander. Use it when you need to recharge your beam battery or as an awareness reminder to shine!

"By listening to
nature's song,
we discover a world
different from our own,
where everything
flows slower, yet always
with purpose."

—LAO TZU

High Tide/Low Tide Meditation

Visit a beach when you know the tide will either be rising or falling.
Sit comfortably and begin this waterside meditation by listening to the
waves as they crash upon the shoreline and align your breath with their
flow. As the tide changes, reflect upon the lessons the water is trying to
share with you. How is the flow? How is the rhythm? How does it align with
your life . . . your celebrations or struggles? Are there any wise water
whisperings, messages, or warnings that are waiting for you to take notice
of them? Are there any worries or wishes you'd like the waters to help
you with?

List any wishes or worries you'd like to share with the waters.
If your life is perfect, then surely, you know somebody
somewhere with a wish or a worry, so this section
should at least have one thing listed. When light beings
aren't working magic for themselves, they are usually
busy sharing their moonbeams with others!

_____

_____

_____

_____

_____

_____

_____

_____

_____

_____

_____

_____

_____

_____

_____

_____

_____

LIST ANY GUIDANCE YOU RECEIVE FROM YOUR
WATERSIDE MEDITATION.

EXAMPLE: Watching the water flow rhythmically by reminds me that it's
a-okay to pace myself. Watching the darker waves, I observed feelings of
stillness, discomfort, and frustration without moving to fix anything.
A brighter wave followed each dark wave. Even though I was feeling
overwhelmed and depressed, it was a treasure to find brightness in a dark
hour. Seeing the waves reflecting light on the surface is a reminder for me
to shine as I drift along.

_____

_____

_____

_____

_____

_____

_____

_____

_____

_____

_____

_____

_____

"EVEN A SMALL STAR
SHINES IN THE DARK."

—Proverb

It's dark in here right now
The lights are off
I am the only one here
But sitting here, I am not alone

There's chatter in the front room
Constantly
But from where I'm sitting
All is still
All is quiet

I hear every word
I feel deeply—every emotion
And I am floating
Levitating—midair
Time bomb, ticked out
Clock cracked, silent shout
Sit
Watch—mind roam
Sit
Breathe—return home

—In Darkness

ZEN AS F*CK RITUAL

FOR WHEN YOU'RE HURT, MAD, OR ANGRY,
BUT YOU KNOW THAT YOU HAVE A GOOD HEART.

Of course, the everyday, all-day goal is to radiate and experience loving kindness toward all living beings, but let's fast-forward to when a motherf*cker done f*cked up and crossed you. You're on a tear—karate-chopping them down in your mind. Oh, but you're supposed to be super zen and loving in every step and every breath. So, in reality, how do you, a badass, overcome feelings of resentment or disappointment toward others?

First, let's go ahead and establish that you know you are a good-hearted person. Angry, hurt, mad, or not, as a light being you sincerely wish beauty and sweetness to all sentient beings. It is your true nature.

Second, it's okay to start with the pain and discomfort sometimes. So here is a ritual that will walk you through the fumes of disappointment straight back to that good ol' kind and sweet heart of yours.

1. You will need a large bowl and a small bowl.

2. Fill each bowl with water. Once you have the bowls ready, set them side by side.

3. Then, in the box below, write down the subject that's got you pressing the ol' shit button. It's okay for you to write this subject in a single word. (It can be a code word that only you can decipher.)

4. Next, allow yourself to feel the intense and disastrously cloudy
   feelings simmering around the subject, turn to face the darkness, and
   write three words that pretty much sum up the damn thing. These are
   words that have you stirring and spinning. These are the words of fire.

   1.

   2.

   3.

Now that you have those clouds down on paper, write the most favorable
outcome you wish to see that coincides with the word of fire you've chosen.
These are words of water.

   1.

   2.

   3.

5. As you take three breaths, focus on the subject and the first word you wrote. Then, turning to the small bowl of water, dip your fingers in the water while softly whispering the word of fire.

6. Next, lightly sprinkle that very same water into the large bowl and whisper the word of water that balances out the fire. Patiently watch each droplet as it ripples across the large bowl. In the same way these soft waves dissipate and dissolve, you are slowly beginning to weave a resolution spell. Although it may take a collective number of spells to change some tides, every badass knows that you have to start somewhere, and it might as well be some place small. Alchemically shifting your energy by bringing your awareness and attention to just a tiny drop of water opens your heart to countless waves of healing possibilities and outcomes. Life is made up of small moments multiplied to form days, months, and years. Taking a few moments to do an exercise like this helps shift your mindset from going off on someone to using your energy wisely by focusing on changing the situation from within first. Then, you can be grounded and speak with them from a more wholesome and loving place. Sometimes, it feels good to say f*ck 'em to all your worries and disappointments, followed by a power-active word of positivity that shows you the way back to your inner light beams. After all, even when light beings are upset, hurt, or angry, they always find a path to re-center and address others with respect and all the kindness they can muster.

Good morning sunshine,
I hope you woke up this morning
Hugging yourself
(Or someone you love)
I hope you told yourself tales
Of all the sweet things
That are awaiting you today

And for tonight
I hope that fireflies
Line the moonrise skies
Just before
You close your eyes

—A Morning Wish

"You must be the change
you wish to see in the world."
—Mahatma Gandhi

The Morning Mantras
of Exhilaration Bath

From poverty to wars, bombs, and shootings, earth can be a very tough realm to wake up to every morning. Even if your life is perfectly flawless and exploding with joy, this planet is full of enough bullshit to keep you backed up with depression for more than a few lifetimes. Upon waking each morning, a badass takes baths in light beams. Start by grumpily or happily rolling over and giving yourself a giant hug. You've made it to a brand-new day! Then, before even stepping outta bed, say five encouraging quotes, words, or wishes to set the tone for the day to be golden. Just like every meal you eat is first prepared, you must also prepare yourself to face the day by taking a light beam bath. No more just wakin' and shakin' without first some self-love makin'! Start setting the stage for the day. That way if all else goes to hell, at least it started beautifully with a few of your favorite thoughts on your mind.

List five quotes, words, or wishes that can be your morning mantras of exhilaration before you even make it to smelling the coffee beans. These are things that you know will always make you excited to get up and get going.

1.

2.

3.

4.

5.

EXTRA TIDBITS OF INNER SELF—INSPIRED
WISDOM AND KNOWLEDGE:

_____

_____

_____

_____

_____

_____

_____

_____

_____

_____

_____

_____

_____

_____

_____

_____

_____

_____

_____

_____

_____

To set up the next day, try to repeat your morning mantras
before falling asleep at night.

THE PERFECT SELF-LOVE DATE EXPERIENCE

While you're on the self-love train, let's plan out a few perfect dates to treat yourself to an afternoon outing or sunset all by your lonesome. Maintaining a balanced level of kindness to yourself helps light beings stay rejuvenated and able to extend their luminous rays from sea to brightly shining sea. Falling in love can take on endless forms, from your favorite socks to people, plants, and animals, but holding space to shower yourself with hugs and wishes is just as necessary for keeping your inner garden growing. Write two dream dates you'd like to treat yourself to that would allow you to appreciate your own company. Vow to enjoy this sacred time alone.

EXAMPLE: I am going to be on a work trip next month. My hotel is very near the river, and my flight will land in time for me to walk down and watch the sunset. There is a delicious taco spot I'll pass along the way. I'll order takeout and a yummy cup of iced fruit tea or mini bottle of Prosecco. I'm definitely going to snag a lovely chocolate bar or dessert as well. I'll sit for an hour or so quietly watching the colorful sunset from a new town. While I'm sure there will be people jogging, walking their puppies, or parents getting in the last few seconds of playtime with their kids, I'll be there alone and quite happily so! This a very important date I've planned to treat myself to before I get busy with work and back in the buzz of the week.

PERFECT SELF-LOVE DATE #1

_____

_____

_____

_____

_____

_____

_____

_____

_____

_____

_____

_____

_____

_____

PERFECT SELF-LOVE DATE #2

_____

_____

_____

_____

_____

_____

_____

_____

_____

_____

_____

_____

_____

_____

_____

_____

I wonder if the moon
Ever halfway questions
If it will make it
Across the sky.

And if a flower
Ever almost open
Worries
How long it will live or die

And if the earth
So gently spinning
Ever wants to turn around

Or if the sun
So brightly shining
Longs to hide and not be found

—A Doubting Moon

Moon Phase #2

Moon Phase #3

Moon Phase #1

Who would disagree that the moon was born to shine? What would happen if the moon started to rise and got halfway across the sky only to drown in a sea of doubt that it could even complete the night's journey? The same is true for you. Somehow, we find it easy to doubt that our life has a purpose and that we have a commitment to practicing light. You were born to shine!

While we may never know how long a particular moment to blossom and shine will last, isn't it worth it just to flower even if only for one night? Though some may bloom for longer than others, where would earth be without flowers?

List any doubts you currently have that are prohibiting you from shooting like a superstar across the midnight sky.

_____

_____

_____

_____

_____

_____

_____

_____

_____

_____

_____

_____

_____

_____

_____

_____

_____

_____

_____

_____

_____

_____

_____

_____

List a few reasons to transcend those doubts.

_____

_____

_____

_____

_____

_____

_____

_____

_____

_____

_____

_____

_____

_____

_____

_____

_____

_____

_____

_____

_____

_____

_____

If it's difficult for you to fully see yourself shining your ass off, then make a list of a few people in your life who may also receive the benefits of you living luminescently. Who would be elevated and inspired by your light? If you can't shine for yourself, can you at least shine for them?

_____

_____

_____

_____

_____

_____

_____

_____

_____

_____

_____

_____

_____

_____

_____

_____

_____

_____

_____

_____

_____

_____

"If the Sun and Moon
should ever doubt,
they'd immediately go out."

—WILLIAM BLAKE

Things Learned from Breathing

I have learned
To be nicer in the mornings
(even though I am not a morning person)
I have learned
To listen — though I love to talk
To be still — when to run, fly, soar —
To walk
I've learned
To cry at different temperatures
Sometimes so hard that the earth will quake
Sometimes so soft a sleeping baby won't wake

I've learned when to give
Learned when to take
When to pray
And when to meditate
How to lose
And how to let go
How to fail
To dream,
To wish,
To hope
From all I've learned
All I know is that
I don't know
But I am willing to live
To die
To grow.

"To know what you know
and what you do not know
is true knowledge."

—Confucius

List five to ten things you are curious to learn more about while you are here on earth. Next, choose one thing from the list and allow your curiosity to run wild. Spend the next few months learning as much as you can about the subject. It's easy as we get older to safely stay in the world we know, but there's always so much more to learn. A badass is never too old to grow.

_____

_____

_____

_____

_____

_____

_____

_____

_____

_____

THE TEN-MINUTE RULE

List ten new or old hobbies you'd like to dive into but haven't found the time. Choose one from the list and dedicate ten minutes to exploring it more each day. Only ten minutes is enough to begin. Multiply that by twenty years, and you're golden!

_____

_____

_____

_____

_____

_____

_____

_____

_____

_____

_____

_____

_____

_____

_____

_____

_____

_____

_____

_____

_____

"ONE SHOULD BECOME THE MASTER OF ONE'S MIND
RATHER THAN LET ONE'S MIND MASTER HIM."

—Nichiren Daishonin,
THE MAJOR WRITINGS OF NICHIREN DAISHONIN, VOL. 1

I USED TO RACE MY MIND
TO THE NEXT MOMENT
HOPING I'D GET THERE FIRST

NOW I AM
IN THE MOMENT
WHERE MY MIND MEETS ME FOR AFTERNOON TEA

I LISTEN TO ITS CONSTANT CHATTER
AS WE BOTH SIP AND SMILE
AND WHEN IT'S EAGER TO OVERTAKE ME
I WATCH—LETTING IT RUN WILD

—Matters of a Monkey Mind

Our minds wander endlessly and continuously. When we watch a movie, there's no way to crawl into the screen and become a part of the cast. We can only observe. Imagine your mind is a movie.

MIND AS A MOVIE EXERCISE

Allowing your mind to be a movie, watch as it moves from scene to scene. Without becoming a cast member in all of its daydreams and wanderings, write a love letter to your mind. Send love to any far-out thoughts that don't align with your light as well as all of the thoughts that positively resonate with you. Examine the good, the bad, and the ugly with a detached point of view. As the observer, you might find your mind to be quite an entertaining character.

DEAREST WANDERING MIND,

_____
_____
_____
_____
_____
_____
_____
_____
_____
_____
_____
_____
_____
_____
_____
_____
_____
_____
_____
_____
_____
_____
_____
_____
_____

With Love from Me,

_____

"IF YOU CATCH A FALLING LEAF," SHE SAID
"THEN YOU GET TO MAKE A WISH."

AND SO OFF WE WENT
WITH RED, YELLOW,
DEEP ORANGE,
AND GREEN
WHIZZING BY
SOARING, SPINNING, AND TWIRLING 'CROSS THE SKY
OFF WE WENT—RIDING
DANCING
ON THE WILDNESS OF THE WIND.

—*The Wildness of Wind and Wishes*

"TO SET FIRE TO THE WOOD,
YOU NEED THE HELP
OF THE WIND."

—Tibetan proverb

LESSONS IN LETTING GO

Have you ever tried with all your might to fix a problem that just doesn't seem to have a bright outcome or solution? While the oak tree may be ready to shed its leaves for the winter, perhaps the maple tree is not quite there yet. What happens when the seasons change and a tree is not yet ready to let go? Every season of our lives comes bearing new lessons. Fall is an excellent time to remember how to let go. Sometimes, when we let go, we find the answers we were looking for all along, but letting go can be very difficult. For those of us who like control, it feels like sliding down a hill in mud. The next time fall comes into your life be sure to take some time for this exercise. For every time you let something in your life go, you are just as easily guaranteed to receive something new in its place. Letting go is a time to simultaneously make wishes. It's the universe inviting us to dream a new dream.

FALL LEAF CATCHING EXERCISE

Venture outside on a fall day (to a space that is safe and free from cars zooming by). Watch as leaves fall from the trees that are ready to let go of their summer bounty. I dare you to try to catch a falling leaf. Go on! Give it a try. For every leaf you catch, you get to make a wish. Let each leaf you catch represent bravely dreaming a new dream.

FALL LEAF CEREMONY

Collect ten or more fall leaves. Write a single inspiring line, goal, word, or wish on each leaf. Use the leaves as seasonal decorations around your house or office.

GRIEVING HEART-RIPPED SIDEWALK MEDITATION

It's impossible to be an earthling and avoid times of discomfort. Yes, even light beings feel depressed, sad, heartbroken, abused, or lonely. For many challenges and obstacles, maybe letting go is the path to realizing your natural glow again, but the thorns of some roses are sharper and tougher to navigate through.

Examine an issue that seems out of your control. Without trying to sort or solve anything, list all the reasons that are making it hard to see the light.

Warning: Creating this list might make you feel super emotional or vulnerable. It is definitely alright to cry and cry like a hard rain on a summer day. Allow yourself to feel what you're feeling without trying to do a damn thing about it. Remember that though the cave you are entering appears to be overwhelmingly cloudy and dark, the light is always bright and present within you. Look inward.

_____

_____

_____

_____

_____

_____

_____

_____

_____

_____

_____

_____

_____

_____

_____

_____

_____

_____

_____

_____

_____

_____

_____

"But only he who, himself enlightened,
is not afraid of shadows."

—IMMANUEL KANT

Begin by simply walking down the sidewalk and bringing your attention to the list you created and the issue weighing you down. With each line in the concrete, take a deep breath in and out. Realize that the answer at this time may be that there is no answer. There is comfort in trusting that you don't always have to see and know the way. You just have to take one step at a time allowing the day to unfold. Notice your shadow as you move from place to place. The light is always with you. You are not alone. How else would the shadows be created? This exercise can be done quickly, if you have some place to be, or slowly. Choose your own pace. Only you can determine the timing that is most divine for this inner exploration.

"ABOVE THE CLOUD WITH ITS
SHADOW IS THE STAR WITH
ITS LIGHT. ABOVE ALL THINGS
REVERENCE THYSELF."

—Pythagoras

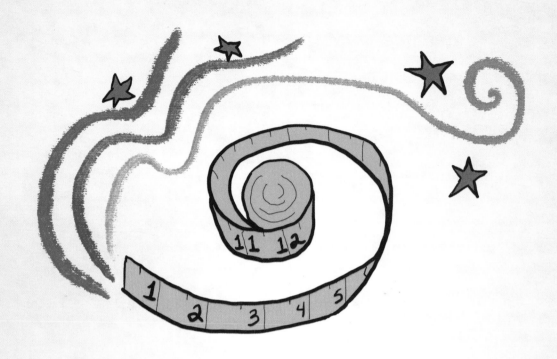

Of nature's rhythmic radiance
Of time's harmonious cadence
We flow in melodic sun dance
Intertwined by symphonic happenstance

Of winter's frost-glazed wonder
And spring's moss-grazed thunder
Perceived by a countless number
Let no being be put asunder.

—Immeasurable Effervescence

What does it mean to shine?

You have a birthright to shine. Shining is a decision to be kind to yourself and others. It's a decision to choose joy even though you might be filled with sadness. A spirit's natural way is lightness of being and joy. No one can ever take your natural glow. It's nature's gift. Just as we watch the seasons change, we can also observe friends, co-workers, or neighbors as they shine and create wonderful things.

List three people you know personally who are doing things you admire. Send them a quick text, email, or note letting them know how much you appreciate their light.

1.

2.

3.

_____

_____

_____

_____

_____

_____

_____

_____

_____

_____

_____

List three people you do not know personally who are doing things you
admire. Write a note or line here that uplifts them and lets their spirit
know you adore their light. It's a-okay to be a superfan and gush about how
amazing you think someone is from afar. We are all stars!

1.

2.

3.

_____
_____
_____
_____
_____
_____
_____
_____
_____
_____
_____
_____
_____
_____
_____

List three people you may be jealous of who are shining their asses off. Beside each name, write one trait they have that you'd like to have for yourself. Thank them for pointing out something you want to call forth and work on. Wish them well on their journey and uplift them in a Light Beam Visualization Exercise from the opening of this book. All are teachers. All are guides.

1.

2.

3.

_____

_____

_____

_____

_____

_____

_____

_____

_____

_____

_____

_____

_____

_____

"You are the light of the world. A city set on a hill cannot be hidden. Nor do people light a lamp and put it under a basket, but on a stand, and it gives light to all in the house. In the same way, let your light shine before others, so that they may see your good deeds."

—Matthew 5:14-16

It is not meditate or pray.
It's meditate AND pray
Eat and breathe
Sleep and dream
Live and love
Hope and wish
Laugh and dance
Work and play
Meditate and Pray.

—Ways of Being

There are times when our minds become rigid in their ways, thinking that there is only one path or method to achieving an outcome.

Like the poem, list the places in which you see yourself becoming rigid or too timid to allow your joy to expand. You might be telling yourself that if you decide to be a painter, then you can't also become a potter, or if you are a doctor, then you can't also be a skydiving instructor. If you laugh too much, you won't be able to cry when you really need to. But why the hell not?! Why allow rigid mental limits to prohibit you from enjoying all the neat things you'd like to explore while you're on earth?

List any rigid thoughts:

1.

2.

3.

List a lighter, balancing word to soften each hard place.

1.

2.

3.

What could an alternative outcome be? Are there any undiscovered pathways?
How can you find a balancing point to even out the rigid points? How would
it feel to be open to all paths? Anything is possible, and everything
is expanding. Although things may currently feel rigid, allow your
imagination to explore any hopeful possibilities. Allow your mind to be
light and limitless. Believe!

_____

_____

_____

_____

_____

_____

_____

_____

_____

_____

_____

_____

_____

_____

_____

_____

_____

_____

_____

_____

_____

_____

_____

List places you'd like to visit:

1.

2.

3.

4.

5.

List things you'd like to see:

1.

2.

3.

4.

5.

The adventures are just beginning!
May your lightning bolt know no limits!

GATHERING STONES EXERCISE

Gather three stones that are large enough to write a single word on. Take your time gathering the stones. They may be right outside your door or any place you might wander over a longer period of time. You will know when you have the right ones. Choose one of the balancing words that you've written on page 72 as opposites of the hard and rigid, stone-like places you've allowed your mind to create. Write the balancing word on the stone. Hide these stones in places you will find them just when you need to be reminded that a badass can be tough and strong without growing too rigid.

"PIT RACE AGAINST RACE, RELIGION AGAINST RELIGION, PREJUDICE AGAINST PREJUDICE. DIVIDE AND CONQUER! WE MUST NOT LET THAT HAPPEN HERE."

—Eleanor Roosevelt

SOMETIMES LIGHT WORK
ISN'T LIGHT—
WORK—
SOMETIMES
IT WEIGHS HEAVY AND HARD
BUT YOU SHINE ON ANYWAY
THE PLACEMENT IS SET
THE FEAST HAS BEEN MADE
AND YOU TRUST
THAT ALL COLORS, ANY AGE, GENDER, OR BELIEF
WILL COME CROWNED IN CONSTELLATIONS
TO FILL A SEAT
AT THE TABLE.

—A Meal of Moon Pies

"REMEMBER UPON THE CONDUCT OF EACH DEPENDS THE FATE OF ALL."

—Alexander the Great

Bright privilege is the ability to look at your life at any and every turn and recognize the places and moments when you are living in fortune — and I'm not talking about pecuniary and monetary fortune. Bright privilege is purely those heart-rich gifts of sincere love and joy that you can share with any human you encounter. They are your gifts that hardly cost you a dime to share. Every person has a unique brightness and radiance that can be shared with others. It is a bright privilege to carry these special gifts. No other being is able to share exactly the same light that you carry.

Bright

/brīt/

adjective

1. giving out or reflecting a lot of light; shining:

Priv·i·lege

/'priv(ə)lij/

noun

1. a special right, advantage, or immunity granted or available only to a particular person or group:

Bright Privilege
for Racial Harmony

You were born a stardust creature of beauty ready to shine and set up to glow, and oh yeah, there you go strutting down the catwalk of life like it's a soul train dance flo'! I get it. Life is busy, but what about stopping to acknowledge the privileges we enjoy every day? So many of us are blessed beyond measure. We have more than even those living just a few houses or streets away. What does it look like to acknowledge our privileges and our blessings? What does it look like to use our privileges and blessings to uplift and help others?

While there are unique benefits to being the badass YOU are, the structures and systems of society often create obstacles based on outward appearance, race, gender, or class. For example, being a very tall and attractive person might make it easier for you to land a modeling gig for a top beauty ad. Whereas it may be a little tougher for someone else to seal the very same level deal. What are the benefits of being who you are? How can your gifts be used to open doors for others and help create a more equitable society?

Just like every person carries a gift that can bless others, every culture also collectively comes bearing blessings. Consider the relationship with nature of indigenous tribes that teach us how to respect the land. From creative things like handcrafted ceramics to woven fabrics, music, and art, every culture has a gift that makes our lives more beautiful. Without easily opening the gates to experience the gifts of all cultures, earth is out of balance. We need all, every, and any positive light to shine brightly and shine now! The evolution of humanity is at the point of no return when it comes to fearlessly radiating and growing together.

Privilege hardly seems a blessing if it is not shared and if it comes at a painful cost to those around us. While it may seem to be momentarily enjoyable, unshared privilege is a slow and toxic poison that ultimately unbalances the soul and dims your inner light.

What's the use in being rich if you can't share some of the fortune with those you love? Now, imagine for a second that those you love are any and every human on earth. You are a badass who is ready to embody humanity as one big, oddly functional family, so let's courageously make a seat at the table for these awkward and unsafe conversations. Let's be open to using bright privilege as the icebreaker for some of the slippery slopes we have yet to climb.

Individually and collectively, if we can refocus our wishes and awareness toward the world we wish to see, then our inner roots will transcend the limitations that systemic imbalances attempt to impose. Bright privileges are within our control because they stem from inner roots. They are where our true power lies waiting to be activated.

Let's face it — most undeveloped countries are predominantly nations of color. Earth's more prosperous and affluent nations are mostly white. If you are a white person, how can you use your white privilege to inspire and open doors for those who are less fortunate?

Separately, as people of color, we often carry the daily weight of our past and present-day oppression. It can be hard to shift our energy from the heaviness of the traumas we've endured. It's difficult to create a more beautiful experience if we are too focused on our pain. If you are a person of color, despite miles and miles still left to grow, are there more ways we can celebrate the privileges that our ancestors fought and died for?

By distracting us from centering our lives around beauty, joy, and the gifts we could be creating, has our pain been used to keep us in a form of prison? As Audre Lorde mentions, could our pain be one of the master's tools? If so, how long shall our pain be allowed to reign? Could it be possible to transcend the past and allow joy and delight to be a path to true freedom and harmony?

Are there benefits to being who you are, existing in the skin you're in, or living where you live? List a few of the everyday gifts and blessings you are grateful for.

_____

_____

_____

_____

_____

_____

_____

_____

_____

_____

_____

_____

_____

_____

_____

_____

_____

_____

HARMONIOUS EARTH EXERCISE AND CALL TO ACTION

List the bright privileges you currently have that you think you can share with others.

EXAMPLE: At work, I have a pretty great relationship with everyone around me. My opinions carry weight. I can use my bright privilege to help and support co-workers whose voices aren't often heard. I can remember times when I have felt unheard, so I really want to make space for others to feel safe and invited to share their ideas.

_____

_____

_____

_____

_____

_____

_____

_____

_____

_____

_____

_____

_____

_____

_____

_____

_____

Call to Action

Without actively putting our ideas into practice, these lists are just a bunch of hippie shit on paper. This section is a call to action. Write one way you can actively extend your privileges and gifts to someone else. Vow to make it happen!

_____

_____

_____

_____

_____

_____

_____

_____

_____

_____

_____

_____

_____

_____

_____

_____

_____

_____

_____

List the bright privileges you WISH you had
that you could share with others.

EXAMPLE: I enjoy being alone. Sometimes I really wish I was more involved
in my community and with organizing events. I also wish to meet more
friends from a host of diverse backgrounds. It would be so neat to have
dinners at my house with friends from all cultures and races enjoying life
together.

_____

_____

_____

_____

_____

_____

_____

_____

_____

_____

_____

_____

_____

_____

_____

_____

_____

_____

_____

_____

Call to Action

Write a few ways you would put this wish list into action. Make it happen!

_____

_____

_____

_____

_____

_____

_____

_____

_____

_____

_____

_____

_____

_____

_____

_____

_____

_____

_____

_____

_____

_____

_____

_____

_____

List the bright privileges your town or neighborhood has that you'd
like to see shared with others.

My neighborhood is posh. I'm not rich, but I make a decent living
and the city picks up the trash on time. We even have brown compost bins.
Just a few miles away, the streets are not very clean or safe after certain
hours. I really wish the entire city could be cleaner. Honestly, I don't
see why we don't have gardens and flowers on all the city's streets. Maybe
if there were more gardens in the ghettos, single moms and underprivileged
people would not have such a hard time finding healthy food at affordable
prices. Maybe seeing a flower on the way to work or school would shift
someone's day or lift someone's spirit. What would it look like to see
every neighborhood as earth's garden—thriving, clean, and safe? Although
capitalism allows us to have more on one side of the gate, all of the
earth is our home. What does it look like to extend beauty, safety, and
growth to every corner of the town and neighborhoods that are right in our
own region. I allow myself to imagine and dream of a more harmonious and
beautiful world.

_____

_____

_____

_____

_____

_____

_____

_____

_____

_____

_____

_____

Call to Action

Write a few ways you can contribute to enriching the lives of the people in your community who are less fortunate. List any organizations you could volunteer with who may already be trying to make great changes. Vow to donate or get involved!

_____

_____

_____

_____

_____

_____

_____

_____

_____

_____

_____

_____

_____

_____

_____

_____

_____

_____

_____

_____

_____

_____

List the bright privileges your country has that you'd like to see
shared with the rest of the world.

EXAMPLE: The way women are treated in my country has a great influence
on the way women are treated all over the world. It is a bright privilege
in my country for women to be free to write, read, own businesses, and
do anything men and other humans are able to do. I would love for women
throughout the world to enjoy these same freedoms.

_____

_____

_____

_____

_____

_____

_____

_____

_____

_____

_____

_____

_____

_____

_____

_____

_____

_____

_____

Call to Action

Write a few ways you can contribute to enriching the lives of people in other countries who are less fortunate. List any organizations you could volunteer with who may already be trying to make great changes. Vow to donate or get involved! Feel free to do a Light Beam Visualization Exercise around every entity that comes to mind as you imagine this dream.

_____

_____

_____

_____

_____

_____

_____

_____

_____

_____

_____

_____

_____

_____

_____

_____

_____

_____

_____

"THE SECRET OF CHANGE
IS TO FOCUS ALL OF
YOUR ENERGY, NOT ON
FIGHTING THE OLD, BUT ON
BUILDING THE NEW."

—Socrates

Bright Privilege for a Kinder Planet

So, we've established that it's apparent as we look around the planet that some of us are more privileged than others. For some, to have clean water and a toilet would be a dream. For others, to have an automatic dishwasher would be heavenly. Many times, our privileges just depend on where we were born or how we were raised. If you were born in an underdeveloped country, you may not have access to a washing machine. If you were born in a wealthy nation, you may have a washing machine in your house or a laundromat on your block. If you were born in a poor part of town, you might not have access to the same standard of education that more prosperous areas can afford. Recognizing our privileges and advantages in life is important to light beings because we can use them to try to make life that much easier for others.

Sometimes, it can be hard to truly own our privileges because it forces us to see our fortune amid those who are less fortunate. All fortune comes at a cost to someone and though life may be hard for us, there's always somebody, somewhere, facing more hardships and difficulties than we are.

Looking on the bright side, no matter where you come from, bright privilege is available to any and all of us.

Do you consider yourself a brightly privileged person? If so, what are some of your bright privileges?

Even on the shittiest of shitty shitty bang bang days, we all have some way we could uplift or inspire those in our sphere. This exercise is to be used throughout a day in your life. How can you—at the grocery store, in traffic, on the train, at the post office, or any other daily activity—radiate and exercise your bright privilege? This can be a compliment to a stranger that shows you recognize their humanity and beauty, or the way you show gratitude to the person helping you with an errand. It could be deciding to treat another with exceptional respect and kindness despite the constructs of society that might silently shame us for crossing the tracks. These actions may be small, but why not start somewhere?

Write a few light beam practices you feel are reasonable to take with you during your daily activities:

_____

_____

_____

_____

_____

_____

_____

_____

_____

_____

_____

_____

_____

_____

Write a few practices you can use to extend your bright privilege
to others in your sphere:

_____

_____

_____

_____

_____

_____

_____

_____

_____

_____

_____

_____

_____

_____

_____

_____

_____

_____

_____

_____

_____

_____

_____

Write a few practices you can use to extend your bright privilege
to others BEYOND your sphere:

_____

_____

_____

_____

_____

_____

_____

_____

_____

_____

_____

_____

_____

_____

_____

_____

_____

_____

_____

_____

_____

_____

_____

_____

"Beauty is not
in the face;
beauty is a light
in the heart."

—Kahlil Gibran

If you see this, Then you can say You've seen something Beautiful today

— Look for the Beautiful

Let's create a list of badass words that make you feel ready to rise and shine like a rhinestone on a Dolly Parton pantsuit.

Radiant Sparkling Glowing Sharing Abundant
Peaceful Loving Forgiving Kind Resplendent

_____

_____

_____

_____

_____

_____

_____

_____

_____

_____

_____

_____

_____

_____

_____

_____

_____

_____

_____

_____

Choose ten of these words to be your words of affirmation this week.
Any time a cloud of doubt emerges, embrace it as a sign pointing you to
something beautiful. For every cloud, practice immediately shifting your
focus to your chosen words of affirmation by whispering them like mantras
on repeat as you watch the cloud roll away. If you feel so moved, you can
form them into affirmations by inserting the words, "Thank you because
I am now . . .", but even just repeating the single words in constant
rotation will lift and elevate our vibration!

_____

_____

_____

_____

_____

_____

_____

_____

_____

_____

_____

_____

_____

_____

_____

_____

_____

_____

_____

_____

_____

"The beautiful is less
what one sees than
what one dreams."

—BELGIAN PROVERB

BEAUTY
IS A POLITICAL FORCE.
QUIETLY UNDERRATED.
OFTEN MISUNDERSTOOD.
FIERCELY VIOLENT
IN ITS DEFENSE
OF A THING CALLED LOVE
AND A PATH OF PEACE.

—'Tis a Sin to Belittle Beauty

Q:

WHAT IS A DREAM?
WHY DO WE DREAM?
WHAT IF WE FAIL?
IS TO DREAM TO SUCCEED?

A:

TO DREAM
IS TO REACH YOUR DEATHBED
KNOWING THAT YOUR LIFE'S WORK
HAS ALWAYS BEEN
BIGGER THAN YOU.

—Dreaming for Each Other

While we dream for ourselves, our dreams are for others as well. It can be overwhelming to be a dreamer if you think you need to reach some particular destination of success. Is it not okay to dream for the act of dreaming? To follow a dream is a process toward success. When you are driving down a road, even a dead end will lead you somewhere, so why not gas up your lightship and take to the skies?

DREAMS OF ANOTHER EXERCISE

Start with a reflective mindset focused on gratitude for all those in the past who have sacrificed for you. This can be your ancestors, guides, or mentors. List any dreamers who have influenced your life.

Extend that gratitude to all the dreamers whose dreams you enjoy every day. It could be the maker of your favorite dessert and even the toothpaste brand you use. It can be anything that shapes a day of your life. Merrily . . . Merrily . . . Merrily . . . Merrily, Life is but a dream! From the dreamer of your favorite whiskey brand to almost anything we enjoy, it was first just somebody's dream. This is a space to be grateful for a few of your favorite things.

_____
_____
_____
_____
_____
_____
_____
_____
_____
_____
_____
_____
_____
_____

Just as you enjoy the dreams others have created, are there any dreams your life holds that you hope you can leave behind for others to expand upon? How is your dream bigger than you?

_____

_____

_____

_____

_____

_____

_____

_____

_____

_____

_____

_____

_____

_____

_____

_____

_____

"Twenty years from now you will be more disappointed by the things that you didn't do than by the ones you did do. So throw off the bowlines. Sail away from the safe harbor. Catch the trade winds in your sails. Explore. Dream. Discover."

—Mark Twain

I wonder if we are ready
For how sweet it could be
I wonder if we'd be open
To how good life could get

—POSSIBILITY OF BEAUTY

While some beauty is natural, all beauty takes work.

Perhaps there was a time when our basic instincts needed to be guided by living in a fearful survival mode, barbarism, or an animalistic nature. As the first humans on earth, we needed to be on guard against predators or tribes that might bring us harm, but today, in many nations, we are living in a slither of time that might allow us to begin to relate to each other on gentler and kinder terms. We are finally at a tiny blink in time when we can begin to breathe and dream new dreams. It sometimes seems like we have been conditioned to expect something bad to happen. This is a time when we can recondition ourselves to more consciously kind ways of being.

When filling up a weekly calendar, how much time is spent planning for a disaster? Bad shit just happens. We don't have to plan it. So, as we seek to explore the possibilities of beauty, there's no need to worry about losing touch with the darkness. Darkness always has been and always will be. From magnificent cities and towns to carefully thought-out governments and regulations, all human-made reality is created based on how and where we focus our minds, both collectively and individually. Everything we've created was first someone's thought.

Often, our attachments to realities of darkness keep us perpetuating and creating more thoughts of darkness. While it can seem brutally realistic, tough, and macho to focus our attention on the harshness and injustices of our world, it is actually tougher to live with an empathetic and compassionate heart. To face a world of darkness and consciously choose to redirect our energy toward light, joy, and positivity is one of the fiercest things we could ever do.

Living a practice of light beams is hard work that requires gladiator-style heart-work. Injustices and darkness deserve to be observed, but to cling to them for dear life is to make them our reality versus using them as fuel and motivation to create something new and beautiful. It takes great courage to see light in a dark world. Some might even call it a foolish way to live. It requires us to soberly face the brutalities that exist with a 20/20 vision of hope on the horizon only to be proven wrong daily by a world clinging to negativity. Living brightly will never make the headlines as long as our deep attachment to trauma and disaster reigns, but if we are to create anything other than the same dark experiences, then we've got to begin to use our imaginations. We must begin to imagine more global unity. We must begin to put more energy into bravely dreaming dreams of hope. We must begin to imagine the world as we wish to create it. They say "be careful what you wish for, it may just come true." Well, I sure as hell hope so if we are collectively wishing and focusing on a joyful and harmonious existence for all living beings.

The exercises throughout this book are light beam practices for rejuvenation and strength. These practices are important because light beings face so much toxicity from living in a world that chooses to cling heavily to promoting darkness and fear.

It is dangerous and wild to live brightly in a dark world. It can feel as if everything is working against you and like you are dodging daggers at every turn but shine on anyway, you crazy diamond. F*cking shine ON! Though you may have many unanswered questions and though you may not be able to see how the shift of positivity and joy can truly happen to our planet, shine on. Our job is not to know how, but to plant positive wishes and seeds in every moment and with every atom of our existence. The question is, are we ready for the world to become more harmonious and beautiful? What makes us so afraid to explore avenues of happiness or joy? Are we okay living with this fear of how sweet things could become and how gentle life on earth could be, or are we ready to water the seeds of an elevated earth? If we are ready, then we must enter a realm of wonder, dreams, and imagination in order to call it forth. See it, be it!

What can you imagine? What do you wish to see?

List a few positive shifts you believe humanity is ready to explore. It's a very hopeful process that begins in our minds first. Where we focus our minds is a source of power and strength, so even being open to the thought can be a step in a brighter direction.

EXAMPLE: Imagine there is plenty of food, affordable health care, and basic resources for all.

_____

_____

_____

No one is more important
Than me
There was no one before me
There will be no one after me
Because I see ME AS WE
And what is done to you
Is done to me
We are the flowers of an eternal tree
We are the roots of an eternity
The wings of a butterfly
And everything we can see
So if I bring harm to you
Then it brings harm to me.
We've always been
And we will always be
Through living lives this way
We shall all be free

—Me as We

What would true freedom look like for all human beings? Do you believe
we have ever had a time in the history of humanity to explore the
possibilities for positivity and beauty in the world? If you are a woman,
can you see yourself in male energy? If you are a man, can you see yourself
in female energy? Can you see yourself in those who don't identify as male
or female? If you are young, are you respectful of those who are old? Is
there something beautiful about all races? Do all cultures have something
magical to share? How important is it for us to appreciate the brightness
and gifts of other cultures, races, and beings? Is it something we just do
naturally? How would it look to express our appreciation of this great,
big, and color-filled world we keep spinning on? How important is it to
actively show our love and respect for others?

This is an agreement and vow to honor all colors of humanity.

What country or cultural heritage were you born into?

What is your racial identity?

What is your gender?

Fill in the blanks on the following pages.

Interchange the colors of humanity in the agreement to reflect your life.

Colors of Humanity Agreement

EXAMPLE

I am a loving and kind, stardusty, sparkling <u>Black/African-American Female</u> life
                              (Race)-(Country or cultural heritage)-(Gender)

who loves and respects

ALL stardusty, sparkling <u>red</u>, <u>yellow</u>, <u>white</u>, and <u>brown</u> lives.

Therefore, it is my bright privilege as a badass being

To actively protect and **express** love and respect to **ALL** human lives.

Signature: _____

Date: _____

Colors of Humanity Agreement

I am a loving and kind, stardusty, sparkling

_____ life

who loves and respects

ALL stardusty, sparkling _____,

_____, _____,

and _____ lives.

Therefore, it is my bright privilege as a badass being

To actively protect and express love and respect to ALL human lives.

Signature: _____

Date: _____

"When we try to pick out
anything by itself,
we find it hitched
to everything else
in the Universe."

—John Muir

Continuing to respect the diversity of all human life and seeing all humans as light beings, we must also seek to align ourselves with nature. As a plant mom and nature lover, I look at the shifts happening to our planet, and while I worry about how climate change is affecting humanity, I'm also very concerned about how it is changing plant life. Severe and extreme shifts in the weather will cause heavy precipitation, wind disturbance, heat waves, and drought. All of these events cause stress to plants of every kind. If you have a houseplant, you know how sensitive many plants are to changes in their environment. Many times, when we think of the negative effects of climate change, we only think of how it will change human lives. Stepping outside of our selfish perspectives, we can begin to see how important it is that we think of all living things in relation to the changing climate. While Earth is approximately 4.5 billion years old, and though Mother Earth always manages to survive, many species of plants are becoming extinct. This is an agreement that connects our awareness back to the earth and atmosphere.

PLANETARY CONNECTION AGREEMENT

Oh Lavender, blowing in the wind

Dearest bees, trees, ants, and butterfly friends,

Radiant sun, mystic moon, planets, and stars,

To countless other things I have daily taken for granted

As a human life enjoying the bright privilege of your presence,

I, _____, pledge to henceforth

Honor your life as if it were my own. Your existence matters.

We are one.

Forevermore.

Signature: _____

Date: _____

Location: <u>The Super Badass Planet Earth</u>

With the changing climate, list any habits you can shift
to become more climate conscious.

_____

_____

_____

_____

_____

_____

_____

_____

_____

_____

_____

_____

_____

_____

_____

_____

_____

_____

_____

_____

_____

_____

If you had the power to activate a progressive climate policy or a green energy plan initiative, what would it look like?

_____

_____

_____

_____

_____

_____

_____

_____

_____

_____

_____

_____

_____

_____

_____

_____

_____

_____

_____

_____

_____

Create your own planetary agreement or wish for unity, growth,
and harmony.

_____

_____

_____

_____

_____

_____

_____

_____

_____

_____

_____

_____

_____

_____

_____

_____

_____

_____

_____

_____

_____

_____

_____

_____

_____

"THE ADULT LOOKS TO DEEDS,
THE CHILD TO LOVE."

—Hindustani proverb

What will you tell your son?

Don't tell him that there are drugs to make you shine.

Or that most people cheat,
Get away smooth,
And think it's fine.

That we all carry the seeds
—both the devil and god sow

That there are hidden dangers in the depths
Of almost every soul.

But he must see it as it is
And he must
Choose
To grow
He must take the book that's bound
And beyond it long to know
Of the softer,
Of the sweeter,
Of the fragile,
Gentle, honest, kind,
Of the shifted, Ever present, Elevated mind.

—Elevated Mind

What advice would you give your younger self? Connecting with your inner child, list any guidance you would give to elevate, enlighten, and brighten the days ahead.

_____

_____

_____

_____

_____

_____

_____

_____

_____

_____

_____

_____

_____

_____

_____

_____

_____

_____

_____

_____

_____

_____

No one can take your shine
When you put it on
From the inside out

—WITHIN

"TO AN OPTIMIST EVERY WEED IS A FLOWER;
TO A PESSIMIST EVERY FLOWER IS A WEED."

—*Finnish proverb*

When we stop to wonder how the hell those who have suffered atrocities
and injustices throughout their lives were able to find a reason to hope
despite the bullshit they faced, there is one tried and true reality
inherent to every human born. That reality is your ability to shine. No
matter what life may throw your way, a job loss, closed doors, the death
of a loved one, or any other form of suffering, the joy you have within can
only be taken if you allow it to be. Shine can never be taken. Shine can
never be stolen. Shine can only be given.

Who are you giving shine to?

_____

_____

_____

_____

_____

_____

Rose Petal Shine Ceremony

You will need a rose with petals big enough to write on and your favorite pen.

Make a list of people you are happy giving your shine to.

Beside each name write a word of adoration that makes you think of that person.

Delicately pull a petal off the rose for each name you've written.

Softly write the word of adoration for each person you adore sharing your shine with on the petal.

Create a sanctuary by either arranging the petals in a display bowl for your counter or sliding them in places around your house like between the pages of a book or in your sock drawer. Any time you look at the petals, remember to send hugs to the people you adore. These are words of beauty. Light beings are always leaving behind secret reminders to shine for others or themselves to stumble upon.

_____

_____

_____

_____

_____

_____

_____

_____

_____

Ritual for the Death of a Loved One

It's human nature to feel sad or depressed with the loss of a loved one. For this ritual, light a candle and sit someplace comfortably.

Reflect on the life of the one you've lost. It's okay to cry.

Take a few deep breaths and begin to surround the spirit of your loved one with light. Visualize them protected and surrounded by beams of light. As they are making their transition, there is always time to give them a wish for peacefulness. Even if they've been gone for many years, there is always time to give them your light and your wishes for a gentle transition. Sharing our shine is a never-ending process. It doesn't stop just because something or someone is no longer in the physical form.

"Better to light a candle than
to curse the darkness."

—Chinese proverb

LIKE FINDING A PIECE OF GOLD
IN YOUR OWN BACKYARD

LIKE CATCHING A PRISM'S COLORS
REFLECTED ON AN UNFAMILIAR FLOOR

OR SPOTTING A FOUR-LEAF CLOVER
WHILE WALKING DOWN THE STREET

—*Surprises All Along*

WHAT TREASURES HAVE
BEEN WITH YOU ALL ALONG?
SOMETIMES YOUR LIGHT IS
RIGHT IN FRONT OF YOU,
BUT IT TAKES A WHILE TO SEE IT.

WATER PRISM EXERCISE

Create a water prism by filling a glass dish with water. Place a mirror in the dish at an angle. Find a sunny area to reflect the sunlight through the water. Enjoy the rays of light that have been made possible with only a few ingredients. Ingredients that have been with you all along.

"HITCH YOUR WAGON
TO A STAR."

—Ralph Waldo Emerson

It's hard to fix a problem
Looking only through
A black-and-white lens
Sometimes you need
A moon- and starlike
Point of view

—MESSAGES FROM INNER STARDUST

135

If the stars were to whisper to you, what would they say? The next time you doubt how incredibly wonderful you are as a badass human, remember that you are stardust. When life looks black and white with absolutely nothing but problems in between, challenge yourself to see things from a starlike point of view. Red is the longest wavelength of light that humans are able to see; violet is the shortest. But other creatures like bumblebees or birds can see ultraviolet light, and although we cannot see infrared light, we can certainly feel its heat. Is there anything you've limited to black and white? In examining and reflecting, are there any shades or possibilities you may have missed seeing in between? Stepping into a dusty and gray zone, might your inner stars be trying to show you a glistening new perspective? Write a few lines that reveal an alternative way of seeing something you've seen a million times.

_____

_____

_____

_____

_____

_____

_____

_____

_____

_____

_____

_____

_____

_____

_____

_____

DUSTY SPACE MEDITATION

On a sunny day, sit near a window.

Watch as dust moves through the air like a comet in the night sky.

Notice how it sparkles. Notice how it shines.

Notice how it dances in the space between the windowsill and any other physical thing nearby. This is a practice for remembering to include a starlike option in our toolbox of possibility. After all, we are made of star stuff. If the dust can sparkle, then so can we!

List your reflections and observations after gazing at the sparkling dust. Although it is gritty and around us every day, how is it a reminder of the radiance each moment holds?

_____

_____

_____

_____

_____

_____

_____

_____

_____

_____

_____

_____

There was one who often wondered if the dark days
Would ever go away
Then came a shifting of his gaze
A door was opened to a secret place
And it had been there all along
Just waiting to be glimpsed
Amongst the great unknown

—REVELATION

We can't experience light beams without having spent days crawling in the dark. Oftentimes, our lives can be full of super lows and that's just a part of being an earthling. Maybe the darkness we've known never really goes away, but we just learn how to live with it. Not every day is going to be without f*ckups, failures, or losses. The next time dark days come along, be kind to yourself. Cry if you need to cry. Our sorrows are often an indicator to create or call forth something brighter, something sweeter. When you view everything as a door, then you've learned how to successfully fail. As one path ends in bittersweetness, other avenues begin to reveal themselves.

Successful Failure Exercise

While sitting with the disappointment of a loss or failure, write down one small thing this day held that was amazing. It can be tiny and small but full of enough light that you noticed it!

_____

_____

_____

_____

_____

_____

_____

_____

_____

_____

_____

_____

_____

_____

_____

_____

_____

_____

_____

_____

If you're in a place to take this workbook with you, write down anything amazing that strikes you as it crosses your path. Although it won't change the heaviness you may feel, begin to practice seeing how losses may be doors to seeing things from a new perspective. Both light and dark exist simultaneously, so though you may be overwhelmed, it's okay to allow yourself to see them both.

_____

_____

_____

_____

_____

_____

_____

_____

_____

_____

_____

_____

_____

_____

_____

_____

_____

_____

_____

_____

_____

_____

It can be easy to feel alone in our successes or failures, but no matter who you are or where you are from, everyone has a dream at some point in their lives. Many of our dreams were inspired by those who have come before us. While our pathways are uniquely our own, we are never all alone. We are always standing on the shoulders of both the successes and failures of the trailblazers who have passed this way before. What are some dreams you have that were inspired by your ancestors or historical figures?

_____

_____

_____

_____

_____

_____

_____

_____

_____

_____

_____

_____

_____

_____

_____

_____

_____

_____

_____

_____

"IT TAKES TIME
TO BUILD CASTLES."

—Irish proverb

Q:

WELL, HOW LONG WILL IT TAKE?

A:

IT WILL TAKE
AS LONG
AS IT TAKES.

—To Flower

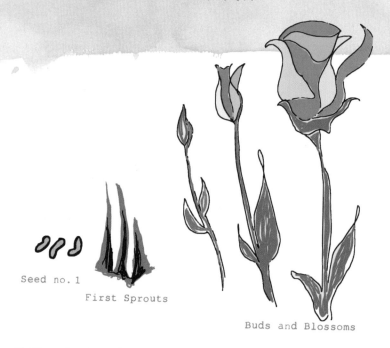

Seed no. 1

First Sprouts

Buds and Blossoms

You can add Miracle-Gro, but ultimately, you can't tell when a flower will bloom. A seed is not concerned about when it will flower or bear fruit. A seed is busy being a seed. There's something to be said for appreciating where you are on the dreamer's path.

FLOWER OBSERVATIONS EXERCISE

It is amazing how many of us live years and years on earth without being able to identify a few flowers that bloom every year in our neighborhood. It's just as important to know a few details about native plants as it is to know how the systems of our government work. Whenever you notice a new flower, take a photo of it. Try to acquire a collection of ten flowers.

Using a plant identification app, determine the name of each flower. Find out if it's a perennial or an annual. Does it require full or partial sunlight? Use this collection of flower images as a guide for those days when you are feeling impatient with your life and wanting something good to happen like yesterday. Remember that everything is in its proper time, and soon you will blossom and soon you will shine. Enjoy being where you are in the process! Be careful! Learning to identify plants can become very addictive.

"Always remember,
you have within you
the strength, the patience,
and the passion
to reach for the stars
to change the world."

—Harriet Tubman

Anywhere
There is a crack
In the concrete
May you find the strength to grow
Fiercely face life's
Trials and troubles
Reaching for the sunlight's glow
And though the world might not be ready
Trust your path because you know
That to flower takes great courage
Mountains move for those who sow.

—*Bravely Believing*

Hard Place Observation Exercise

Now that you have your chosen flower photos, your eyes may be keen to spot flowers anyplace you roam. Observe the odd areas you find where plants are thriving. Have you seen random flowers growing from less fertile conditions like between the cracks in the concrete as you walk along? List a few places plants have grown that occur to you as odd or hard places to grow.

_____

_____

_____

_____

_____

_____

_____

_____

_____

_____

_____

_____

_____

_____

_____

_____

_____

Road Map to Success Exercise

Create a road map to success.

What is an old wish or dream that came true for you? It can be huge or tiny. It only has to be something that you wanted and actually received.

_____

_____

_____

_____

_____

_____

_____

_____

What is a new wish or dream you hope will come true for you?
It too can be huge or tiny.

_____

_____

_____

_____

_____

_____

_____

_____

_____

_____

_____

_____

_____

_____

_____

_____

_____

_____

_____

_____

_____

_____

_____

List any external obstacles you foresee that might make it difficult
to manifest this new wish.

_____

_____

_____

_____

_____

_____

_____

_____

_____

_____

_____

_____

_____

_____

_____

_____

_____

_____

_____

_____

_____

_____

List all internal obstacles you foresee.

_____

_____

_____

_____

_____

_____

_____

_____

_____

_____

_____

_____

_____

_____

_____

_____

_____

_____

_____

_____

_____

What is the timetable for your wish to come true? Whatever number you write, multiply it by ten because life happens, and time will have its way. Although it may happen sooner, a dreamer must calculate for it all. It's a way to realistically handle any resistance, setbacks, or disappointments. Who knows?! After reflecting on the dream from all angles, you may even dream a new dream or invite a team to help you create it. No matter what, never stop dreaming!

_____
_____
_____
_____
_____
_____
_____
_____
_____
_____
_____
_____
_____
_____
_____
_____
_____
_____
_____
_____

List any people you respect who have achieved something you admire.
This is your list of mentors and leaders who keep you inspired.
Feel free to list rivals or enemies as well. Sometimes, they are
your greatest motivators or teachers. Welcome them.

_____

_____

_____

_____

_____

_____

_____

_____

_____

_____

_____

_____

_____

_____

_____

_____

_____

_____

_____

_____

_____

Lastly, list five reasons to believe in your wish or dream today.
These reasons may grow or change as your dream changes, but it is always
a treat to see where it all started.

1.

2.

3.

4.

5.

_____

_____

_____

_____

_____

_____

_____

_____

_____

_____

_____

_____

_____

_____

I will take
The well-lit road
Not by lights
But by the voice of my soul
And choose the path
Of unresolved pain
And teach myself how
To dance in the rain
And I'll be soaked — wet
Before I get home
But at least I'll be singing
My life's truest song

—LIFE'S TRUEST SONG

"Every heart sings a song, incomplete,
until another heart whispers back. Those who
wish to sing always find a song. At the touch
of a lover, everyone becomes a poet."

—Plato

Songs, Sounds, and Silence Exercises

If you had to choose one song to represent your life, what would it be?

Write a line from three of your favorite songs.

_____

_____

_____

_____

_____

_____

_____

_____

_____

_____

_____

_____

_____

SOUNDS.

If you could choose one sound to bring your awareness back to the truest essence of your light path, what would it be? This will be your sound for visions and change. It can be a train whistle, a church bell, the wind against a window, the ding of a text on your phone, or birdsong. Whatever you choose, allow it to shift your attention and bring your awareness back to your light purpose on earth. You may be in the middle of crossing the street in traffic, but when you hear your sound, you will remember to refocus your attention. Allow it to shift your mood and re-center your focus. Allow it to inspire you to be respectful even of those who get on your last nerve. It is the sound that grounds you and brings you back home.

SILENCE.

Noise pollution is a fact of our lives. Take a few moments to sit in silence. How silent is your silence? Write down anything you hear during your moments of silence.

_____

_____

_____

_____

_____

_____

_____

_____

_____

_____

_____

_____

_____

_____

_____

_____

_____

_____

_____

Note to Self: Try to encourage at least thirty seconds of conscious silence in your circle and life each day. Even fifteen to twenty seconds of conscious silence can shift your energy like a lightning bolt in the middle of a thunderstorm or the glimpse of a rainbow from a moving car window.

"Life is a song,
sing it.
Life is a struggle,
accept it."

—Mother Teresa

I'll take today
And tomorrow, too
Just feeling lucky
To spend a lifetime
With you.

—Collecting Yesterdays

NICKNAME EXERCISE

Make a list of people you feel grateful to have in your life. Then, add a loving nickname to those close to you on your phone. Any time their number pops up, you will see the affectionate name you've chosen for them. It can be as simple as adding one of your words of inspiration to their name.

EXAMPLE: "Ama the Wise," "Charlie-Adventurer," "Nina-Illuminate," or "Tommy-Starlight"

_____

_____

_____

_____

_____

_____

_____

_____

_____

_____

_____

_____

_____

_____

_____

_____

_____

_____

"WHAT'S IN A NAME?
THAT WHICH WE CALL A ROSE
BY ANY OTHER NAME WOULD
SMELL AS SWEET."

—William Shakespeare

As the petals
Prepare daily
For the flower,
So the dreamer
Must gently labor
For the dream.

And though some petals
Might not live to see the hour
They pass knowing
Their toils lead to blossoming.

—ANATOMY OF A DREAM

ANATOMY of a DREAM

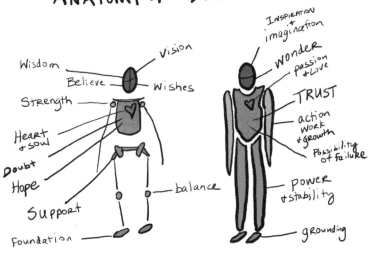

Wisdom
Vision
Believe
Wishes
Strength
Heart & soul
Doubt
Hope
Support
Foundation
balance

Inspiration + imagination
Wonder
passion & Love
TRUST
action work & growth
Possibility of Failure
Power & stability
grounding

Dreaming is a precarious business. Fear of failure can keep us from even entertaining the idea of a new adventure. Just like anyone else, a badass accepts the challenges of dreaming and examines all possibilities of personal failure.

There are so many types of dreams. Some dreams are just for you. Some are for your family or friends. Some are for your country, and some are for the world. Sure, it's not exactly reasonable to believe that every single dream you have will come true in your lifetime, but why should that stop you from dreaming? While you might achieve the dream of an ice-cream sandwich after work or the ideal vacation on the beach, you might not reach the dream of world peace before you croak. Is that a reason to stop dreaming? Do we only dream for ourselves, or are our dreams creating a staircase to the sun that others can climb and build upon? Must every plant produce a flower in order to be beautiful? Though a dream may not become fully realized within your lifetime, every dream is possible. Even when we achieve the dream of ice cream or a vacation, we are helping to activate the dream of someone else. There is an interconnectivity found by dreaming. The world is created by dreamers. A badass knows that dreams are always bigger than one person and considers the fact that, yes, they may not reach the goal intended, but would others be able to benefit and be inspired if they set out on the road anyway? Imagine that you are fortunate enough to live your dream or just to even hold a hobby. Who would you love to leave your dream in the hands of to carry it on long after you are gone? How can your dream be bigger than you? How can it touch the hearts of others? Who would you love to inspire?

"THE MOON
MOVES SLOWLY,
BUT IT GETS
ACROSS THE TOWN."

—African proverb

I was knee-deep
I was all in
I had forgotten
How to begin
Beginnings are wonder-filled
A marvel of mind
Everything glistens,
Glitters, and shines
Time is so dusty
With the gentlest wind
Cloud coughing
Prairie storm
Tunnel no end
Light to awaken
Corner to round
Sleepy eyes open
True treasures found.

—End to Begin

Beginnings can be intimidating, but they are also very exciting. For example, when you first fall in love with a person or thing, everything is filled with wonder and possibilities. There are adventures around every corner. After a little time passes and the glamor fades, it can be hard to tell the glitter from the dust. Although time may have had its way, when you love something it's new every day. Take a look at the things you love. It can be your plants, your bed, a sweater, career, lover, this day, your mama, or your best friend. Write a few wonderful old things and several beautiful new things that make it so adorable. Just because a lamp is old doesn't mean its light is any dimmer than it was before. Sometimes you just have to put on your badass cape and stir up the dust to see the glitter again.

END TO BEGIN EXERCISE

_____

_____

_____

_____

_____

_____

_____

"To be a star, you must shine your own light, follow your path, and don't worry about the darkness, for that is when the stars shine brightest."

—Ralph Waldo Emerson

Of all the things
That I could be
For every ship
Out on the sea
With every flaw and
Darkest night
I'd simply long
To be a light.

—The Lighthouse

Inspiring Dreamers and Light Beings!

This book would not be possible without the decades I've spent examining the revolutionary works and creativity of these powerful and wizardly light beings. I encourage you to explore, research, and study everything they have bravely shared with our brightly shining human family.

Toni Morrison	Gloria Steinem	John Prine
Audre Lorde	Thomas Edison	Elizabeth Cotten
bell hooks	Paul Ferrini	Precious Bryant
Thich Nhat Hanh	Betty Friedan	Algia Mae Hinton
Alice Walker	Andy Warhol	Swamp Dogg
Octavia Butler	Esther Hicks	Skip James
W. E. B. Du Bois	Kerri Kelly	Holly Bass
Sun Ra	Carl Jung	Robert Johnson
Alice Coltrane	Shonda Rhimes	The Carter Family
Carl Sagan	Isabel Wilkerson	Elvis Presley
Hafiz of Shiraz	Robin Wall Kimmerer	Charles Chaplin
David Bowie	Noam Chomsky	Billie Holiday
Paramahansa Yogananda	Ibram X. Kendi	Louis Armstrong
Pink Floyd	Yayoi Kusama	Tina Turner
Clarissa Pinkola Estés	Ta-Nehisi Coates	Maya Angelou
Zora Neale Hurston	Robin DiAngelo	Amanda Gorman
Wendell Berry	Joyce Kilmer	Kendrick Lamar
Harriet Tubman	Oprah Winfrey	Bob Dylan
Joseph Campbell	Dalai Lama	Pete Seeger
Valarie Kaur	Desmond Tutu	Sojourner Truth
Yuval Noah Harari	Howard Thurman	Eckhart Tolle
James Baldwin	Langston Hughes	Whitney Houston
Miguel Ruiz	Howard Zinn	Paulo Coelho
James Allen	Jimi Hendrix	Louise L. Hay
Kahlil Gibran	Sister Rosetta Tharpe	Deepak Chopra
Jean-Michel Basquiat	Little Richard	Shakti Gawain
Ram Dass	Mississippi John Hurt	Jane Roberts

Mahatma Gandhi

Serena Williams

Venus Williams

Marina Abramović

Nelson Mandela

Otis Redding

Doreen Virtue

Lao Tzu

Confucius

Hazrat Inayat Khan

Carla Thomas

Vaneese Thomas

Dr. Martin Luther
  King Jr.

Mother Teresa

Jesus

Malcom X

Sam Cooke

Caroline Myss

Pema Chödrön

Buddha

Prince

Fela Kuti

Nina Simone

Muhammad Ali

Neil deGrasse Tyson

Aretha Franklin

Stephen Hawking

Brian Greene

Frederick Douglass

Rhonda Byrne

Henry David Thoreau

Angela Davis

Rosa Parks

Ralph Waldo Emerson

Jeffrey Robinson

Georgia O'Keeffe

Paul Laurence Dunbar

Osho

Phillis Wheatley

Tricia Hersey

Alex Haley

Kurt Cobain

Augusta Savage

George Orwell

Eleanor Roosevelt

Michelle Obama

Frida Kahlo

Ida B. Wells

Fannie Lou Hamer

The Staple Singers

Mister Rogers

Rep. John Lewis

Albert Einstein

Richard Bach

Marilyn Monroe

Medicine Cards

Aristotle

Bob Marley

Chief Seattle

Dolly Parton

Dr. Seuss

George Lucas

Jim Henson

Johann Wolfgang
  von Goethe

John Muir

Leonard Cohen

Mark Twain

Plato

Socrates

William Blake

Emily Dickinson

Mary Burns

John Lennon

George Harrison

Neale Donald Walsch

J. R. R. Tolkien

Bill W.

Dr. Bob

William Shakespeare

Rupi Kaur

Jen Sincero

James Brown

Marianne Williamson

Alan Watts

Monica Sweeney

Carlos Castaneda

Ray Charles

Julia Cameron

Brené Brown

Walt Whitman

Gary Zukav

Shel Silverstein

Daniel Quinn

Amma

Ocean Vuong

Jacqueline Suskin

Krista Tippett

Tupac Shakur

Rumi

Our ancestors and countless other radical light beings
who surround us every day!

Acknowledgments

I am positively overwhelmed with gratitude for all of the light beings who inspired this book. Thank you to my family and friends for being the sparkling stars lighting up the moments of my life. To my mother, June, and my badass sisters, Kayla and Jasmine, y'all keep me on my twinkling tippy toes. To my brothers Jason and Patrick, your strength and courage is like fireworks on a holiday. To name a few of my bright companions: these words were taking shape while watching the sun rise and set in Bali with Jes Crownover, seeing the Lynn Canyon Waterfall glisten in Vancouver with Ayan Ajanaku, shopping for flowers at Pike Place Market in Seattle with Heidi Knochenhauer, drinking tea in Brooklyn with Tommy Kha, sitting on a porch in Memphis with Njeri Fombi, having wine with Marce, Norah, Emily, and Sarah, sharing art with Sarah Walko and Coco, making dinners with Sally on the beach in Florida, celebrating love with Sheena, Keith, and Grace overlooking the Mediterranean Sea in the South of France, and touring the world with my badass band.

Thank you to my fans, like Philista, Danny, Regina, and Jeff, who always remind me to shine!

Thank you to my agent, Rachel Vogel, for passionately sharing my work and providing feedback along the way.

Thank you to Allison Adler for your dedication and understanding of my words and message. The descriptive text you wrote on the very back of this book made me tear up. I'm so happy it was your last gift to us before venturing on to other publishing worlds.

Thank you so much to my publisher, Andrews McMeel Publishing, for believing in my second book. It is refreshing to work with a team of super badass women: Patty Rice, Danys Mares, Brianna Westervelt, Holly Swayne, Shona Burns, and Cat Vaughn.

To Amanda Lucidon, Alan Spearman, Sister Peace, and the Grounded Team,
I will always be grateful to you for introducing my written words to the
publishing world. From making music to writing poems, there are countless
ways to shine. May our light radiate endlessly.

Thank you to my dear friends in Tuscany for opening up your lovely home for
me to write so many of the nature exercises. I adore Italy and your gardens
filled with fresh lavender, grapes for wine, olive trees, and fresh
veggies lining the Tuscan countryside were the loveliest place to sit and
write.

Thank you to Matt for spending mornings over coffee listening to me talk
about writing this new book full of "hippie sh*t"!

In loving memory of Gran—ninety-six years of shining brighter than the
hot southern summer sun.

To my readers, may this book keep you ever remembering the badass gifts you
came to share with this crazy, wild world.

Shine!

About the Author

VALERIE JUNE HOCKETT is a Grammy-nominated artist from Tennessee. She's been hailed by the *New York Times* as one of America's "most intriguing, fully formed new talents." A musician, singer, songwriter, poet, illustrator, actor, certified yoga and mindfulness meditation instructor, and author, she honorably served as a Turnaround artist working with students for the President's Committee for the Arts and Humanities and continues serving through The Kennedy Center. She has recorded three critically acclaimed, best-selling solo albums and has also written songs for legendary artists such as Mavis Staples and The Blind Boys of Alabama. An Amazon #1 Best Seller in poetry, her first book, *Maps for the Modern World*, is a collection of lyrical poems and original illustrations about cultivating community, awareness, and harmony with our surroundings as we move fearlessly toward our dreams. She is also the author of the children's book *Somebody to Love: The Story of Valerie June's Sweet Little Baby Banjolele*, published by Jack White's Third Man Books. When she's not touring, she splits her time between Tennessee and New York.

DEAR WORLD, THERE IS SO MUCH FUCKING BEAUTY!

—I See You